CHESAPEAKE

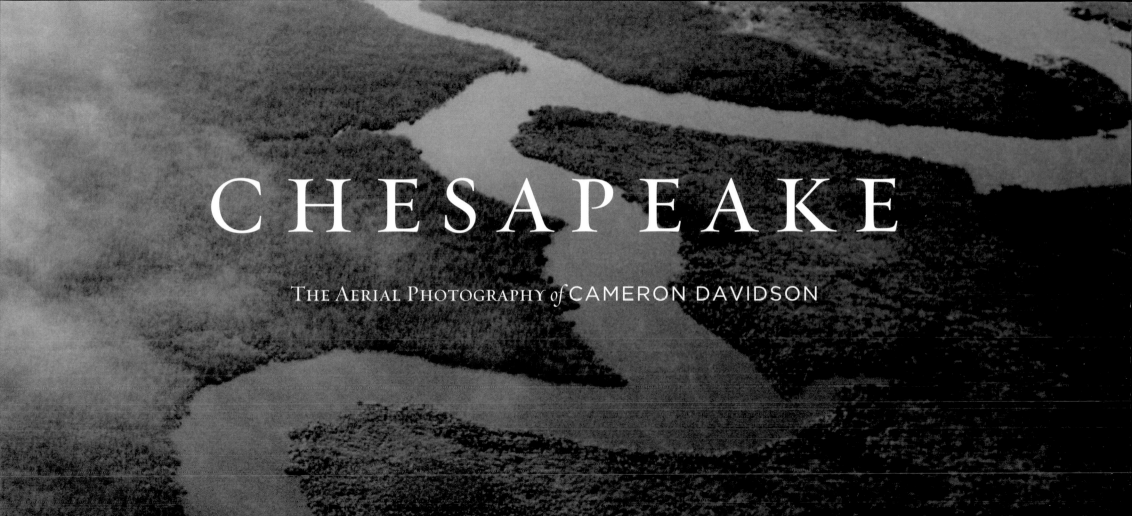

CHESAPEAKE

THE AERIAL PHOTOGRAPHY *of* CAMERON DAVIDSON

PRECEDING SPREAD: Early-morning fog wisps over Jug Bay on Maryland's Patuxent River.

In memory of
SIOBHAN, TOM & JOYCE REYNDERS

FOREWORD

CAMERON DAVIDSON

In 1979, while working on a personal project on great blue herons, I saw a lone Piper Cub sitting on a grass runway along Croom Road in southern Maryland. The plane was next to a farmhouse with an old red barn that served as its hangar. I drove up the driveway, knocked on the farmhouse door, and a middle-aged woman answered and invited me in after I told her about my project.

I asked if it would be possible to charter the aircraft for a photo flight over the Black Swamp Creek heronry; she said to wait just a bit. Her husband, a pilot, arrived a few minutes later. I explained what I was shooting and asked him if it would be possible to fly me for a short while. Cost me 15 bucks, and I was hooked. We took off from this dogleg of a runway that ran uphill. The little yellow Piper climbed quickly and, before I knew it, the three miles between the farm and the rookery were behind us. I was now staring down at the tops of nests scattered throughout a strand of sycamore trees at the foot of a hill and the head of the swamp, all within easy flying distance of the river for the parents of the shrieking great blue heron chicks beneath me. That did it for me. I found my answer, and it wasn't wildlife photography—which I thought would be my life's work—nor was it landscapes. It was the combination of the two. The aerial platform became the perfect vehicle to combine my love of graphic patterns and the grand landscape. The interaction of mankind, the land and water captured my attention over and over again.

Soon thereafter, I was given permission from Robert Gilka, director of photography for *National Geographic,* to charter a JetRanger helicopter from Montgomery County Airpark in Gaithersburg, Maryland, to shoot more aerials of the heronry for my now-approved photo assignment on the birds. The flight along the Patuxent River from its headwaters to Jug Bay, the meandering saltwater marsh that marks the tidal limit of the Patuxent and down the river, became the genesis of this project. On that flight, I discovered I could isolate subjects from an unusual viewpoint and tell the story from a different frame of reference. The patterns I saw began to repeat themselves in every flight I took, from the wandering curves of a creek flowing across a marsh to new suburbs that followed the same patterns with winding roads set within soon-to-fall forests. I am drawn to observing the world with a graphic perspective. It is what and how I see. Even when shooting on the ground for a magazine or commercial assignment, my eye tends to frame my subject within a graphical perspective. My earliest photographs have strong receding lines, shadows or bold colors. Viewing things in this context is perfect for aerial photography. It allows me to frame tightly, remove the subject from the landscape and engage the viewer in a bit of a cat-and-mouse game. What was being looked at? How high was the photograph taken? Often, I shoot without a horizon line in the frame, which enables me to focus all my creative energy on the subject. If I am successful with the photograph, it becomes content first within a frame of graphics, with color and shadow to tease the viewer. My endeavors led me to the Chesapeake watershed. It is vast, stretching from Otsego Lake in central New York State to western Pennsylvania, and south through

Delaware, Maryland, the District of Columbia, Virginia and West Virginia to its mouth separating the Delmarva Peninsula from Virginia Beach. The topography and hydrologic zones plus the human imprint on the land and water interest me. A farmer in upstate New York or Virginia allowing his cattle to wade in a stream can impact the bay downstream as much as an abandoned mine leaching acid into a stream in West Virginia or Pennsylvania. My goal was to shoot the entire watershed from the air, showing a consistent viewpoint—not grand overviews but vignettes of life that, when tied together, present the whole of the bay. I wanted to make visual statements about what is important, why it is necessary to do everything we can to protect it and ensure it survives.

Helicopter and small airplane shots are very different animals. My preference is a turbine helicopter such as a MD 500 or Bell JetRanger. The turbine offers a larger margin of safety, the weight-to-power ratio is greater, plus I find that most pilots who "fly for the camera" prefer turbine ships. I often sit in the back, on the floor, with the door off and a harness on to ensure that I don't make the leap into the great unknown. In a helicopter, it is easier to work with the pilot as a team. He or she sees what I am seeing and, because I am also a pilot, we speak the same language, so my instructions are quickly and easily understood. Likewise, I know to shut my mouth when the pilot is speaking with air traffic control. Rising 50 or 60 feet can dramatically change one's perspective and sense of scale in an image. I like that. I enjoy how I can cover more of a subject from the helicopter than I can in an airplane. In the helicopter, I feel like I am in front of the subject and know when everything will become aligned for that perfect perspective. In an airplane, I typically sit directly behind the pilot. And because it's necessary to stay above stall speed, the flight and steep turns required for a straight-down perspective happen much more quickly. Time after time, I feel I am chasing the image and need to overshoot. It is what it is. Helicopters can fly lower and slower, change altitude easily, and are expensive to operate and charter. Fixed-wing aircraft such as the Cessna 172 are economical but limited to higher altitudes and speeds. Roughly half of the Chesapeake watershed project was shot from a Cessna 177 or an ancient straight-tail Cessna 150. Everything shot low and slow was from helicopters, mostly Bell JetRangers and a MD 500. The lower Eastern Shore aerials were shot from a Robinson R22 trainer, and the James River images were taken from a Schweizer 300 based near Richmond, Virginia.

ABOVE: MD 500 turbine helicopter

8

When I prepare for a shoot, I go through a process of cleaning my equipment and making sure the digital sensors are free of dust, the critical polarizing filters are smear-free and my fast prime lenses are all working properly. My gyroscope is fully charged and ready to smooth out the bumps and roughness of flight. I check the weather, way too often, and I confer with the pilot about what we are trying to shoot and how we are going to plan our flight. The sectional flight charts are laid out, and I imagine the marshes and mountains unfolding below me.

I prepare yet still depend on luck. I need to be in awe-inspiring light to have the clarity and crispness that, these days, is so very rare on the East Coast, except for a few weeks each spring and fall. These are the moments when we are blessed with spectacularly clean light that looks as if it was washed and dried with 50-plus miles of visibility. These are the days I live for, when I can climb to 8,000 feet and see from the mountains of Virginia all the way to Baltimore. I always say a little prayer before every flight for several reasons: I am a bit superstitious, I am religious, and I feel like I am calling upon my inspiration to safeguard my life and to create images worthy of the risk I am undertaking. Every time we lift off, it feels right. I am at home and at peace when I am in the air. A calm settles over me and I become alert to the possibilities unfolding beneath my lens. Even though the landscape of western Pennsylvania has little to do with the marshes of the Delmarva, the connection exists. The kinship is the water that is slowly flowing downhill from the Eastern Continental Divide, across the Piedmont plateau and through the coastal plain to the tidal zone of the bay. The water is what connects us to the bay. We live in the watershed; it quenches our thirst; we play, fish and hunt upon it; we ignore it; and we cherish it. It has always been there. It is a part of our history, and we must protect it, so that it will be here for the future.

ABOVE: Great Falls of the Potomac River in midwinter
FOLLOWING SPREAD: The Blackwater River flows into Fishing Creek from
the Blackwater National Wildlife Refuge on Maryland's Eastern Shore.

UPPER BAY

The upper Chesapeake Bay—the section stretching from the estuary's freshwater umbilical, the Susquehanna River, south to the Calvert Cliffs—is the bay that residents of the Baltimore and Washington regions know best. Watery fingers of the northern Chesapeake reach up to Annapolis's scenic City Dock and curl around the tourist-jammed downtown of St. Michaels. One of the upper bay's branches laps at Baltimore's Inner Harbor, its water both scenic and toxic.

The Chesapeake Bay Bridge crosses from Sandy Point State Park to Kent Island, giving motorists a tantalizing aerial view of the vast estuary. We know this section of the bay so well, in part because we have changed it so thoroughly. Both the watershed and the water of the upper Chesapeake have been heavily remade—for ill but also, sometimes, for good—by people. The uppermost reaches of the Chesapeake watershed lie hundreds of miles from the nearest waterman's shanty, in a cold lake near Cooperstown, New York. Here, the river was permanently widened and deepened thousands of years ago, at the end of the last Ice Age, by melting glaciers and rising seas. From Otsego Lake, the Susquehanna, whose drowned lower reaches form the Chesapeake, gains strength crossing Pennsylvania, and when it empties into the Chesapeake at Havre de Grace, Maryland, it carries 19 million gallons every minute. This single source accounts for about half of all the freshwater that enters the bay.

As it flows, the Susquehanna takes in runoff from farms, suburbs and sewage plants, and so it brings a heavy human influence to bear on the upper Chesapeake. The big river is one of the bay's largest sources of two key pollutants: nitrogen and phosphorus. The same pollutants also flow down from highly fertilized lawns along the Severn and South rivers near Annapolis, and from Eastern Shore rivers tainted with poultry manure. In the bay, these act like underwater Miracle-Gro, feeding algal blooms that deplete the bay's dissolved oxygen. The result, in some places, is "dead zones" where fish and crabs can't breathe. Other problems come from industrial sites such as Baltimore's Sparrows Point steel plant: Here, years of industrial pollution have helped make parts of the Patapsco River a toxic soup.

But if the upper bay showcases the harm that humans have done to the Chesapeake, it has also demonstrated our potential to help. There is less nitrogen coming down the Susquehanna now, a bit of good news that might be the result of cleanup efforts—or maybe just good luck—as a few recent dry years resulted in fewer pollutants washing off the land. Whatever the cause, the improvements in the Susquehanna have triggered a remarkable resurgence in the Chesapeake's upper regions. It happens like this: Less pollution means fewer algae, which means clearer water, which means underwater plants get the sunlight they need. The result of this chain reaction has been the growth of huge grass beds in the upper bay, which provide a nursery for baby crabs and food for waterfowl. These grasses also serve as a natural filter, helping to accelerate the cleaning of the water that brought them back in the first place. Maryland officials say it is possible in some places to see eight feet down into the water. That is unprecedented clarity in an estuary long characterized by murk.

From the air, the wide angles of Cameron Davidson's photographs highlight the human footprint on the upper bay. Farm fields, far up in the Susquehanna's watershed, are marked with lines too straight *not* to be man-made. Cows loll in a stream, leaving waste that will eventually make its way down to the Chesapeake. Church steeples poke up from the trees around a bay tributary. The Sparrows Point steel plant is all smoking pipes and gray buildings, the arteries and arms of an infernal machine. At a waterside development, a geometric pattern of buildings stands out among a green riot of trees.

It is a consolation, however, to know that in a few parts of the upper bay—filtered by thriving grass beds, partially freed from pollution's shadow—the impact of humans might also look like clear water. In other words, like nothing at all.

RIGHT: The Susquehanna River less than a mile from its headwaters at Lake Otsego near Cooperstown, New York—where the Chesapeake Bay begins its meandering, majestic journey.

ABOVE: The lower Susquehanna River in Pennsylvania after the double blizzard of January 2010
RIGHT: Sheet ice shifts downstream on the lower Susquehanna.

LEFT: Contour farmland along Fishing Creek near Drumore, Pennsylvania
ABOVE: Near Fairfield, Pennsylvania, contour farming curves along the northern shore
of the Susquehanna River.

LEFT: Little Hoover and Hoover islands bisect the Susquehanna River across from Fishers Ferry, Pennsylvania, eight miles south of the confluence of the West Branch Susquehanna and Susquehanna rivers at Northumberland.

ABOVE: The Susquehanna and West Branch Susquehanna rivers join near Sunbury, Pennsylvania.

LEFT: Three Mile Island nuclear generating station in Dauphin County, Pennsylvania, near Harrisburg powers up along the banks of the Susquehanna River three decades after a partial core meltdown.
ABOVE: Created by political activist Gene Stilp in 1991, this 25-foot-high replica of the Statue of Liberty lifts her lamp from a pier of the former Marysville Bridge in the Susquehanna River upstream from Harrisburg.

ABOVE: Farm fields near Binghamton, New York, frame the Susquehanna River.

RIGHT: An unnamed creek in northern Pennsylvania puts late fall along the Susquehanna into focus.

ABOVE: A spillway over railroad tracks carries winter's wet bounty to the
north shore of the Susquehanna River south of Harrisburg.
RIGHT: Sun begins to set on the Susquehanna near Paxton, Pennsylvania.

ABOVE: Completed on September 29, 1931, the Safe Harbor Dam in Pennsylvania is one of three hydroelectric dams on the lower Susquehanna River.

RIGHT: Another, the Conowingo Dam in Maryland, see from the southern shoreline of the Susquehanna River, is one of the largest nonfederal hydroelectric dams in the United States.

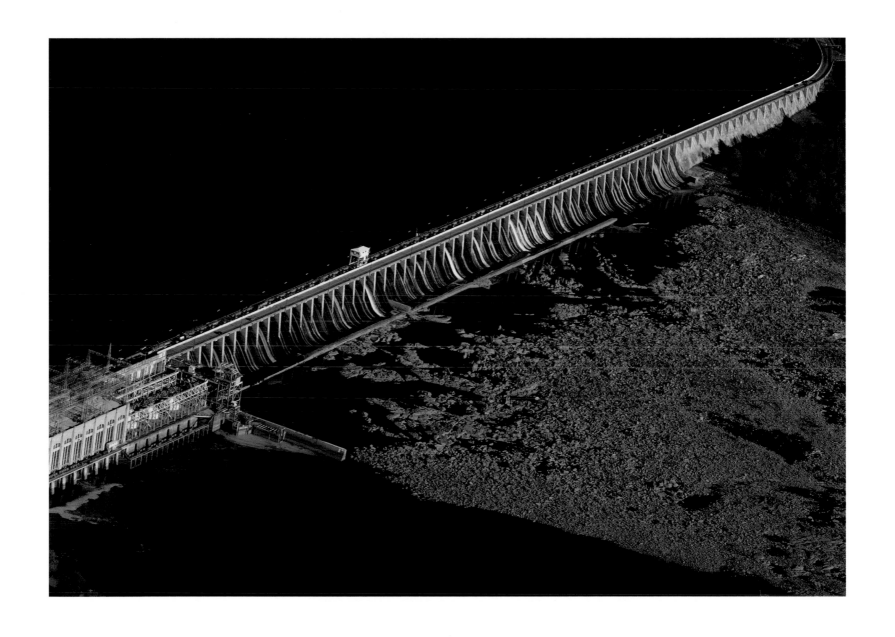

LEFT: This inoperable railroad trestle crosses midpoint in the Chesapeake and Delaware Canal near
St. Georges, Delaware.
ABOVE: A fuel barge pushed by a tug makes its way from Delaware into the bay through the Chesapeake
and Delaware Canal. Canal construction started in 1824 and was completed at a cost of $2.5 million in 1929.

ABOVE: Hydrilla plants gather on the eastern side of a peninsula in the Sassafras River,
in Maryland, with the Chesapeake in the distance.
RIGHT: A grid of homes abuts Buttonwood Beach on Maryland's Eastern Shore.

ABOVE: The Sparrows Point Shipyard Industrial Complex originated in 1887 as Maryland Steel but has had numerous owners since then. The SS *Ancon*, the first ship to sail the Panama Canal, was constructed here.
RIGHT: More of the Sparrows Point Shipyard Industrial Complex in the distance.

NEXT SPREAD, LEFT: Downtown Baltimore and the Inner Harbor at sunrise looking toward the Patapsco River.
RIGHT: The appropriately star-shaped Fort McHenry (with Baltimore in the background) was where Francis Scott Key wrote "The Star-Spangled Banner."

MIDDLE BAY

The middle Chesapeake—which stretches from the Calvert Cliffs down to the Virginia state line—is beautiful and wild, the closest thing in real life to the idealized bay we conjure in our imaginations. The Chesapeake is wide and empty here, reachable from cities only by boat or by a long car ride. In this region, set off in isolation, the crabs still run and the watermen still motor off to catch them. Here, isolated towns still live the old way, fed by the water and comforted by camp-meeting Methodism.

The middle bay can seem like a place where the land just gave up: Its necks and peninsulas peter out into wetlands, then into vast expanses of water. Stand at Smith Point, Virginia, and look north: The Potomac River is 11 miles across. Look east: The Chesapeake is 30 miles across. And, all the time, the water is slowly encroaching and conquering even more territory here. In Dorchester County, on Maryland's Eastern Shore, an area that was once home to farms and villages has already turned to marsh. As sea levels rise, much of it may eventually be swallowed whole, the old tomato fields submerged and covered in eelgrass.

The middle bay's geographic isolation has left its people with some of the strongest cultural links to the Chesapeake's past. On Smith Island—one of only two inhabited islands left in the middle of the bay—the locals speak with a famous variant on the Maryland accent, grown distinct over years of separate living. House sounds like "hace"; brown is pronounced "brain." Even on the mainland, the midsection of the Eastern Shore still feels distant from the urban bustle that flows over the shore's two bridges. This is a place where people still hold "muskrat suppers" as church fundraisers, and where the World Championship Muskrat Skinning Contest is held every year in the tiny Dorchester village of Golden Hill. That contest's uncomplicated rules: "Fastest time, clean 'rat." In the water, however, the middle bay's isolation is not enough to protect its waters from pollution. Here, freshwater flowing downstream from the Chesapeake's tributary rivers brings traces of manure, fertilizer and treated sewage. That means it brings down nitrogen and phosphorus, the pollutants that trigger runaway algal blooms, which leave dead zones in their wake. This process happens all over the Chesapeake, but here it is worsened by a peculiar natural phenomenon: a kind of a floor in the water itself.

In this section of the Chesapeake, colder, saltier water rushes north from the ocean, and warmer, fresher water flows in from the rivers. But sometimes, the two don't mix: They stratify. The salty water sinks to the bottom, and the fresh water sits on top. The boundary between them acts as a kind of barrier: it effectively stops oxygen-rich water from the top layer from mixing with depleted water in the depths. This floor—the scientific term is "pycnocline"—keeps the middle bay's deep sections oxygen-deprived for longer than they would otherwise be.

From the air, Davidson's camera shows the Potomac River's beginnings in steep-sided Appalachian valleys. In the Chesapeake itself, Davidson catches a boat rocketing through a wide, blue sheet of water. His photographs can look like art: patterns in a marsh's creeks and an ice sheet's cracks so complex that they almost appear fractal. And they can look like photojournalism, highlighting the places where man's damage to the bay is most obvious. There is a forest with a bald spot, marred by a clear-cut. A farm-country tributary turned brown by eroding soil and the waste of lounging cows. Together, they show the interconnected processes that make the middle Chesapeake both beautifully wild and soberingly man-made.

RIGHT: A northbound sailboat is dwarfed by the dual spans of the
Chesapeake Bay Bridge from above Sandy Point State Park in Maryland.

PRECEDING SPREAD: The bright lights of Washington, D.C.—from the Kennedy Center to the Jefferson Memorial along the Potomac River—shine from a vantage point above Rosslyn, Virginia.
ABOVE AND RIGHT: Red tide—seawater that becomes toxic from a large amount of algal organisms—flows south on the Rappahannock River near Tappahannock, Virginia.

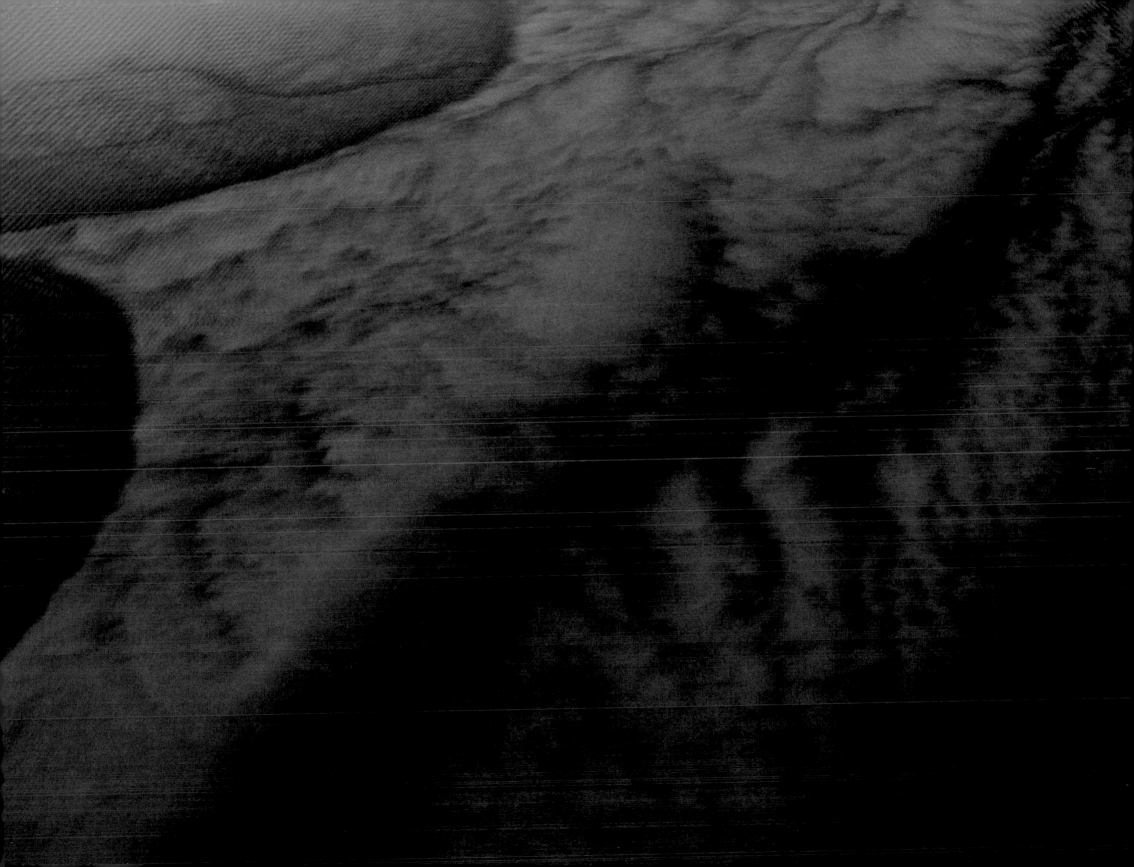

ABOVE: Early-morning fog and clouds reflect impressionistically in the Piankatank River near its confluence with the Chesapeake Bay in Virginia's Middle Peninsula.
RIGHT: The Route 3 bridge spans the Rappahannock River near White Stone, Virginia.

ABOVE: Fog shrouds the Piankatank River.

RIGHT: Islands are rendered as ice floes in the Potomac River in West Virginia.

ABOVE: Jug Bay Natural Area on the Patuxent River in Prince George's County, Maryland,
as the sun sets behind the Potomac River.
RIGHT: Morning breaks on the Piankatank River in the Middle Peninsula of Virginia.

LEFT: River fog conjures a dust bowl along the eastern banks of the Patuxent River in Calvert County, Maryland.
ABOVE: The golden walls of Calvert Cliffs State Park shoreline hug the western shore of the Chesapeake Bay in Calvert County.

PRECEDING SPREAD, LEFT: The Blackwater River winds its way through the Blackwater National Wildlife
Refuge 12 miles south of Cambridge, Maryland, in Dorchester County.
PRECEDING SPREAD, RIGHT: Frozen ice sheets marble the Chesapeake Bay near the mouth of the Severn River.

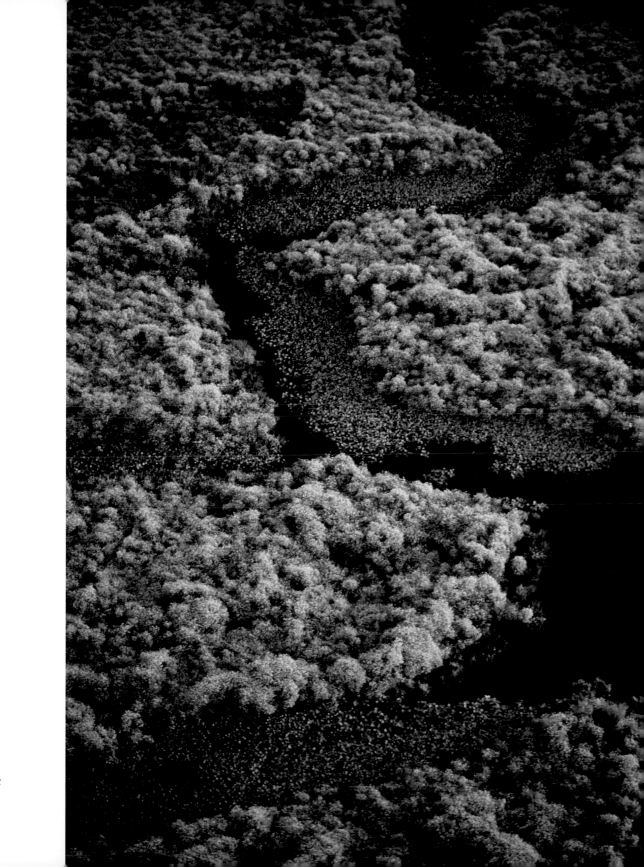

LEFT: Thomas Branch and Grover Creek merge before entering the bay at Calvert Cliffs State Park in Maryland.
RIGHT: Dyke Marsh Wildlife Preserve forms the western shoreline of the Potomac River along the George Washington Parkway south of Alexandria, Virginia.

LEFT: One of the most turbulent parts of the Chesapeake system, Great Falls of the Potomac River in Virginia, churn in the early morning.
ABOVE: The White House, Washington Monument, and Jefferson Memorial nearly align before the Potomac River from above 17th Street, NW, on a snowy and cold December morning.

PRECEDING SPREAD, LEFT: Early-morning fog dots the Jug Bay Wetlands Sanctuary of the
Patuxent River near Croom, Maryland.
PRECEDING SPREAD, RIGHT: Placid Potomac River islands lie upstream from the raucous Great Falls.

LEFT: Outflow from the Choptank River mixes with the Chesapeake near Tilghman Island in Maryland.
RIGHT: In Cambridge, Maryland, mud flats reveal themselves at low tide in the Blackwater River in the
Blackwater National Wildlife Refuge.

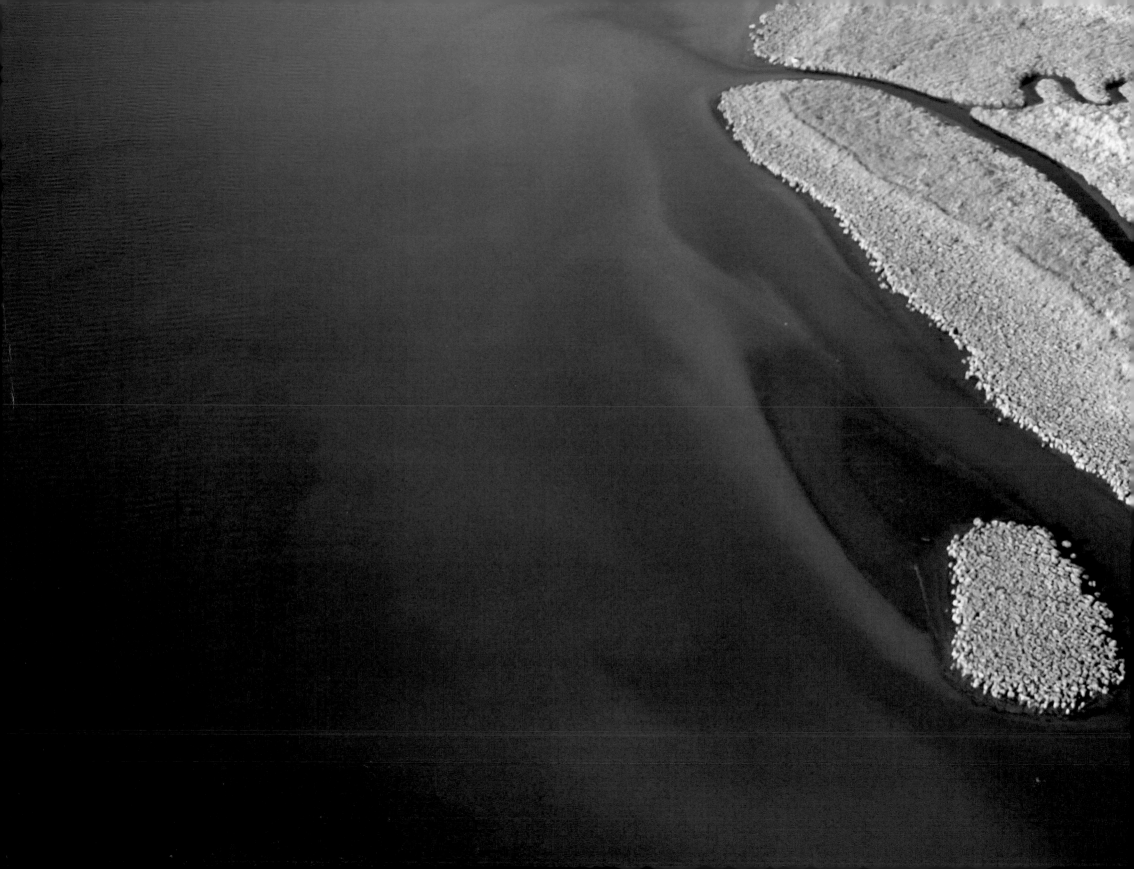

PRECEDING SPREAD: A serpentine creek flows through the Round Island Marsh to the Nanticoke River south of Vienna, Maryland.

LEFT: Sun sets on a frozen Chesapeake near Crisfield, Maryland.

ABOVE: The Potomac River and Goose Creek near Leesburg, Virginia meet to reflect the sun's waning rays.

ABOVE: Frozen midwinter marshes and a wall of clouds create planes over the Tangier Sound.

RIGHT: A late afternoon flotilla approaches the South River in Annapolis, Maryland.

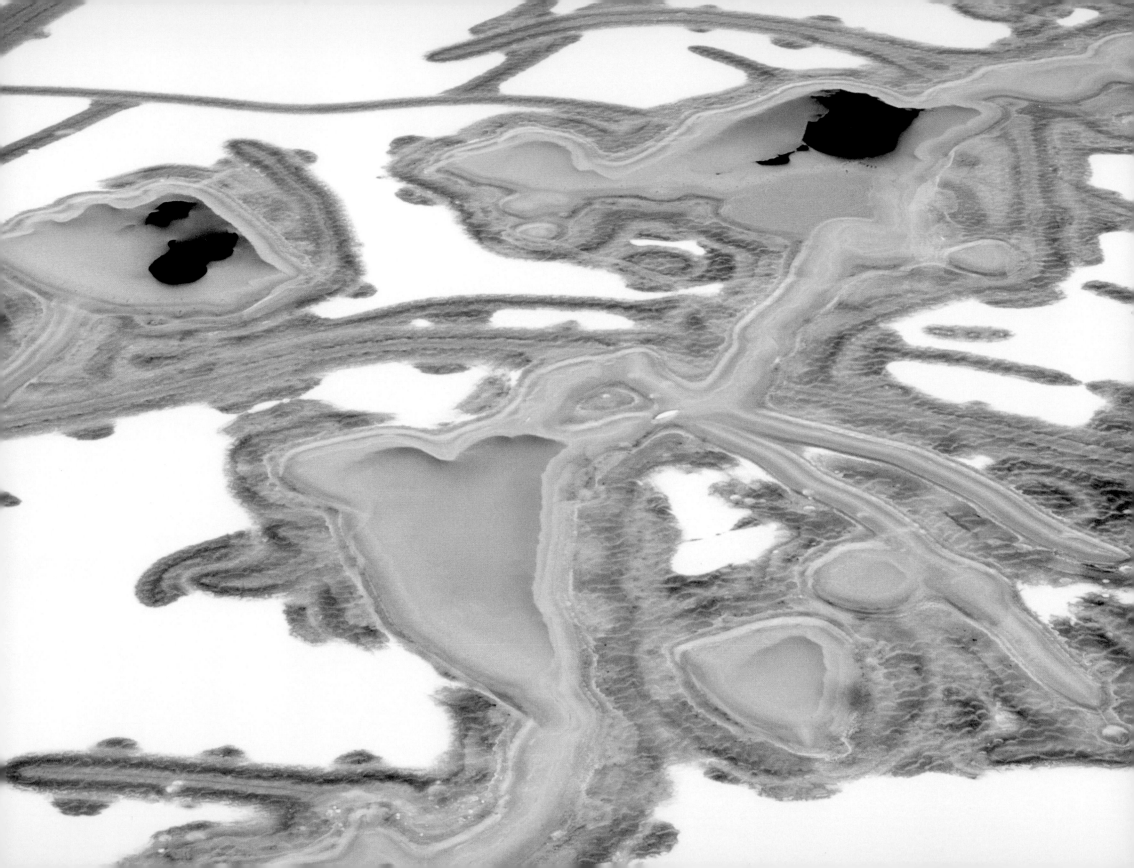

LEFT: Frozen pathways mark the Potomac River near Point Lookout Lighthouse in St. Mary's County, Maryland.

ABOVE: The frozen Chesapeake dips from beneath snow and ice along its western shore, south of the Bay Bridge.

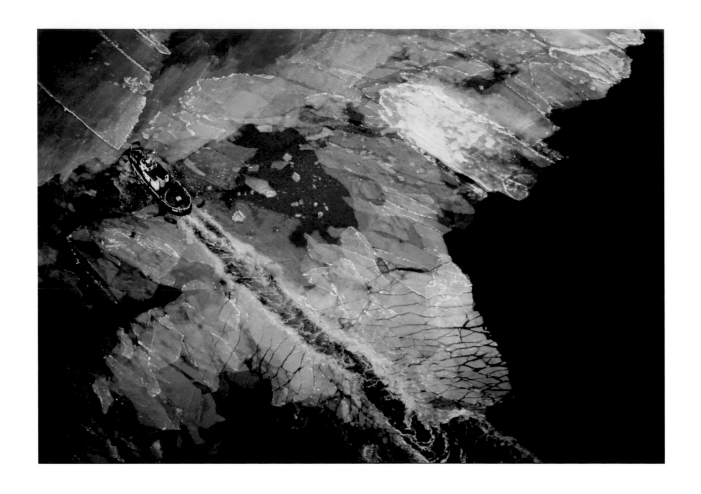

ABOVE: A U.S. Coast Guard cutter creates a channel through the frozen ice of the
Little Annemessex River outflow into the Chesapeake in Maryland.
RIGHT: "Save the Bay," the rallying cry of the Chesapeake Bay Foundation, is carved
in ice on a frozen cove near Annapolis, Maryland.

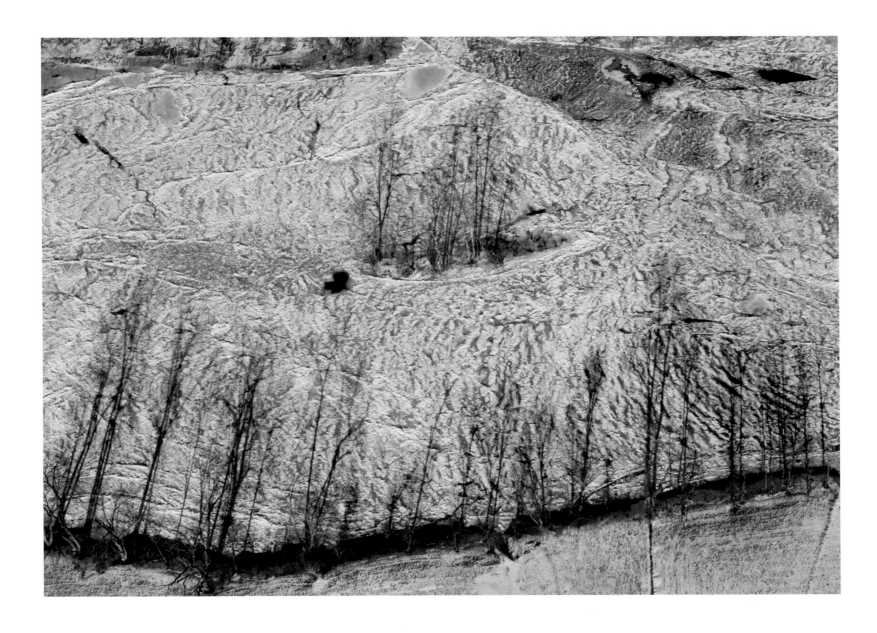

ABOVE: Ice clogs the South Fork of the Shenandoah River near Bentonville, Virginia.

RIGHT: The many shapes of the South Fork Shenandoah in midwinter near Rileyville, Virginia.

LEFT: Catch basins square off at a poultry farm on Maryland's Eastern Shore in Queen Anne's County.
ABOVE: A Queen Anne's County farm near the Eastern Shore

LEFT: Frozen marshes seemingly float above the Cedar Island State Wildlife Management
Area near Pocomoke Sound on Maryland's Eastern Shore.
ABOVE: The waterlogged northern tip of Bloodsworth Island and Tigs Cove.

LEFT: Construction is begun on a new housing development along the Potomac River in Fairfax County, Virginia.

ABOVE: The Maryland State House in Annapolis is the third building constructed on this site. The first was destroyed by fire in 1704; the second was razed in 1769. Construction on this building started in 1772 and was finished 27 years later.

ABOVE AND RIGHT: A tributary of Linville Creek meets livestock on a farm in Broadway,
Virginia before flowing into the Shenandoah River.

LEFT: The "seven bends" of the North Fork Shenandoah River, near Woodstock, Virginia are all captured from 8,500 feet on a January afternoon. The river flows north along the edges of the George Washington and Jefferson National Forests to its confluence in Front Royal with the South Fork Shenandoah.
ABOVE: Some of the seven bends from 6,000 feet in midsummer.

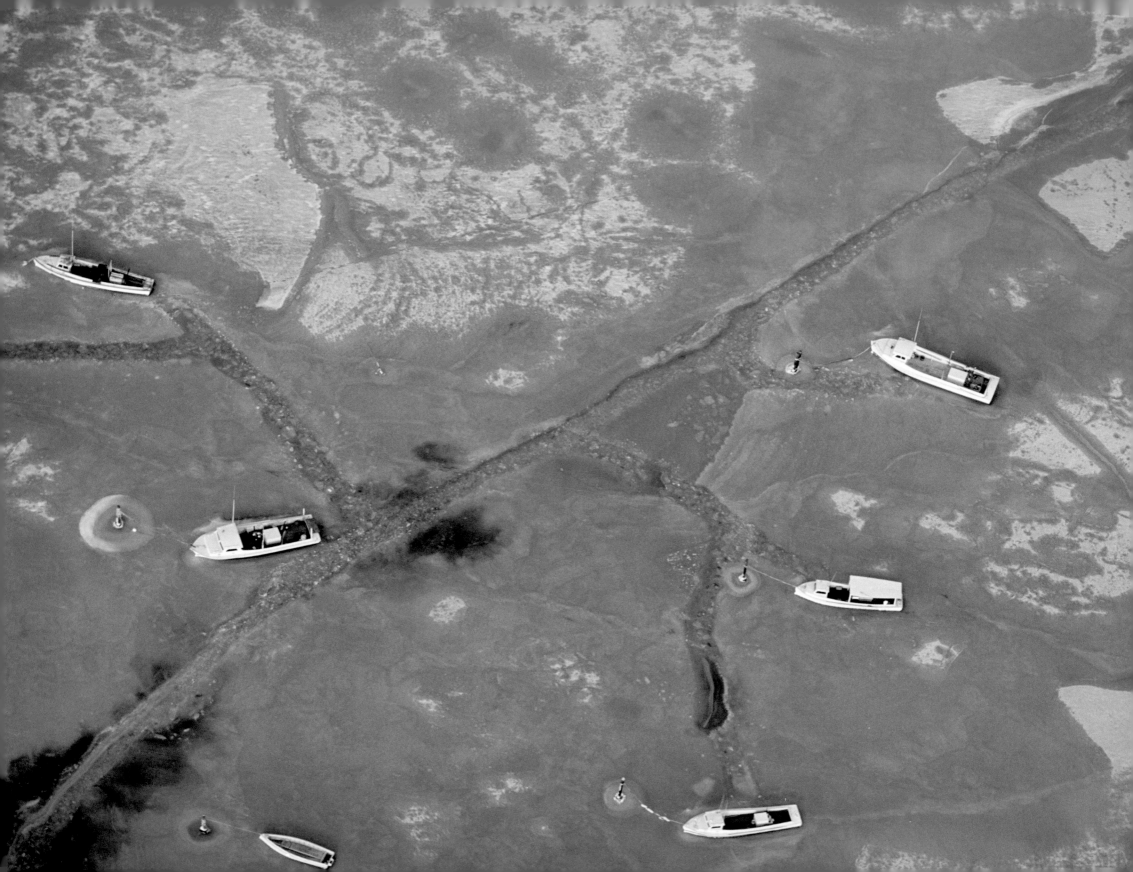

LEFT: Work boats lie at anchor in the frozen ice near Deal Island on the Eastern Shore of Maryland.
ABOVE: The frozen Patuxent River harbors a flock of Canada geese in southern Prince George's County, Maryland.

LEFT: The North Fork of the Potomac River's South Branch flows past lush farms in Pendleton County, West Virginia.

ABOVE: Harpers Ferry, West Virginia, a national historical park and site of the infamous John Brown raid, marks the confluence of the Shenandoah and Potomac rivers.

ABOVE: Oil floats on water in a marsh along the northern shore of the James River near Williamsburg, Virginia.
RIGHT: Fog cloaks the Northern Neck peninsula of Virginia in late fall.

LEFT: On Bloodsworth Island, Maryland, a former bombing practice range for the United States Navy, great blue heron now range from these nesting platforms.

ABOVE: Blackwater River rolls into Fishing Bay adjacent to the Blackwater National Wildlife Refuge.

PRECEDING SPREAD: An isolated house stands on the edge of marshes along Maryland's Eastern Shore.

LEFT AND ABOVE: Marshes on the northern shorelines of Fishing Bay and Blackwater National Wildlife Refuge on Maryland's Eastern Shore graphically portray the cuts that research scientists used to test water flow in an attempt to control mosquito populations.

THIS PAGE: Union Maj. Gen. Ambrose Burnside's troops captured this stone bridge over Antietam Creek in Maryland during the Battle of Antietam on September 17, 1862. Antietam Creek is said to have run red with the blood from Confederate and Union casualties.
RIGHT: A boardwalk crosses the Patuxent River at the Merkle Wildlife Sanctuary in Prince George's County, Maryland.

ABOVE: Hoopersville Bridge transits the ice-crusted Cat Cove and Honga
River at Hoopers Island on Maryland's Eastern Shore.
RIGHT: Marshes near Bloodsworth Island in Maryland

LEFT: In 1847, Poplar Island covered more than 1,000 acres; by 1990, it accounted for less than 10. The U.S. Army Corps of Engineers and the Maryland Port Administration started reconstructing it in 1998 with dredged material from the Baltimore shipping channel, a two-decades long project.

THE
LOWER BAY

The lower Chesapeake—Virginia's bay—is defined in an ecological sense by salt, by the Atlantic rushing into the estuary with the tide. Culturally, the region is defined by history and harbors, by connections to the ocean and places beyond. Here, the metropolis is Hampton Roads, a region named for the watery byways that surround it. Supported by the U.S. Navy and commercial shipping, this cluster of cities still makes its living on the water in a way that Washington and Baltimore do not.

Looking north from Hampton Roads, the lower bay's western shore is all peninsulas. Virginia's great rivers widen as they approach the bay here, leaving the necks of land between them physically isolated and culturally distinct. Between the Potomac and the Rappahannock, the Northern Neck is home to a Deep South accent and the plantations where Robert E. Lee and George Washington were born. Between the Rappahannock and the York, the Middle Peninsula is rural enough to hide a near-pristine Chesapeake tributary—Dragon Run—in its center. Farther south is the historic Virginia Peninsula, between the York and the James. There, it is only a short trip from the remains of the Jamestown settlement to the advancing edge of urban sprawl.

To creatures living in its waters, the lower bay is the gateway to the Atlantic, largely shaped by the encroaching salt water. It is the place where pregnant female crabs overwinter, buried in mud, ready to release their millions of eggs into currents that will carry the eggs out to sea. It is the place where Chesapeake oysters are designed to thrive: The bivalves can live anywhere in the bay, but they reproduce most successfully in saltier water. It is a part of the bay with fewer dead zones than others: The ocean water brings in fresh oxygen to replace that lost to pollution-driven algal blooms. But human influences can still make the lower Chesapeake's biological engine sputter and seize up. For years here, crabs were scraped out of the winter burrows by watermen, taking their eggs from the water unhatched. Lower-bay oysters were decimated by diseases that humans seem to have brought in inadvertently. An industrial-fishing operation based in Reedville, Virginia, takes vast amounts of menhaden—a small fish that filters the bay's water as it feeds—to be ground up and processed into fish oil. And, despite the ocean's flushing, sections of the lower Chesapeake have been heavily polluted. The Elizabeth River was cursed by its capacity as a natural harbor: Industry clustered around it and left its bottom polluted and its fish ridden with tumors. Environmentalists at the Elizabeth River Project said the only solution was to take the contaminated mud away: "Goo Must Go!" Now, new policies are changing this place. In two Virginia rivers, the Lynnhaven and the Great Wicomico, new government and private projects (aided by favorable weather) have re-created thriving oyster reefs. Virginia recently banned the wintertime dredging of crabs and reduced its overall crab harvest in concert with Maryland. And, on the Elizabeth, the goo is going. It is being dredged out and taken to landfills in a multimillion-dollar project that began in the summer of 2009, paid for by both public and private sources. In pictures, the lower bay's human signature leaps out of the frame.

On the James River, the Ghost Fleet—a dwindling group of old merchant ships held by the government in floating reserve—crowds together in midstream. In Hampton Roads, the bridge-tunnel complex that connects to the Eastern Shore is a long arc over water and islands. In Virginia Beach, bathers crowd the sand. But Davidson's camera also finds pristine-looking marshes and river valleys.

One of this section's most beautiful shots reveals people and nature coexisting. It was shot in the clear light of midwinter: Below, on Virginia's Tangier Island, churches, homes and an airport crowd the three remaining spines of dry land. Here, on the tiny island, watermen have drawn their living from the Chesapeake since the 1600s, sustained by a bay that—then—must have seemed endless and invincible.

RIGHT: Looking west across the Chesapeake Bay Bridge-Tunnel offshore from Fisherman Island, Virginia.

LEFT: A creek meanders through the marshes of Presquile National Wildlife Refuge
on the James River of Virginia.
ABOVE: Extreme low tide near Wilsonia on the lower Eastern Shore of Virginia.

PRECEDING SPREAD: Markings along a marsh near the mouth of the Chesapeake and the Eastern Shore of Virginia
LEFT: The southern tip of the Eastern Shore of Virginia and Fisherman Island

LEFT: The headwaters of the Pamunkey River in central Virginia
ABOVE: Fox Island, Jamestown Island and the James River in Virginia

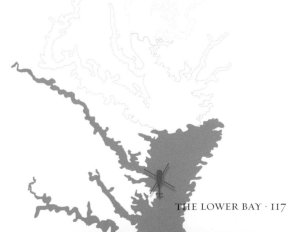

LEFT: Bay meets sea off Virginia Beach, where container ships lie at anchor before entering the lower Chesapeake.

ABOVE: A Maersk Sealand container ship with pilot tugs gets thrust to its berth in Portsmouth, Virginia.

LEFT AND ABOVE: The U.S. Navy stores the Ghost Fleet—the National Defense Reserve Fleet, a flotilla of decommissioned vessels—in the James River upstream from Newport News. These ships are considered an environmental disaster in the making because many contain oil and fuel that might leak.

PRECEDING SPREAD: River fog rises at sunrise along the James River near Elk Island, Virginia.

ABOVE: The villages of Ewell and Tylerton on Smith Island as seen from 3,500 feet.

ABOVE: A mere 604 residents of Virginia's Tangier Island were counted in the 2000 census. The Tangier dialect is unique in the Chesapeake region and is connected to 1660 Restoration English.

LEFT AND RIGHT: The James River passes lazily through a hazy Blue Ridge Mountains.

ABOVE: Yorktown Battlefield in Virginia is where Gen. Lord Cornwallis, commander of 6,000 British Troops, surrendered to Comte de Rochambeau of France and Gen. George Washington, who together commanded 16,600 troops at the Battle of Yorktown on October 19, 1781.

ABOVE: Fort Monroe guarded the channel passing from the Chesapeake Bay into Hampton
Roads during the Civil War. A Union fort surrounded by the Confederacy, it became the
home of escaped Southern slaves who settled into "contraband camps."

LEFT: Marshes of the Chickahominy River meander half a mile upstream from its confluence with the James River.
ABOVE: Motorboats on the Pamunkey River in late spring race near the Pamunkey Indian reservation in central Virginia.

ABOVE: Near Fisherman Island on Virginia's lower Eastern Shore, fishermen gather their catch from a pound net.
RIGHT: The 17.6-mile-long Chesapeake Bay Bridge-Tunnel connects Virginia Beach with the Eastern Shore of Virginia.

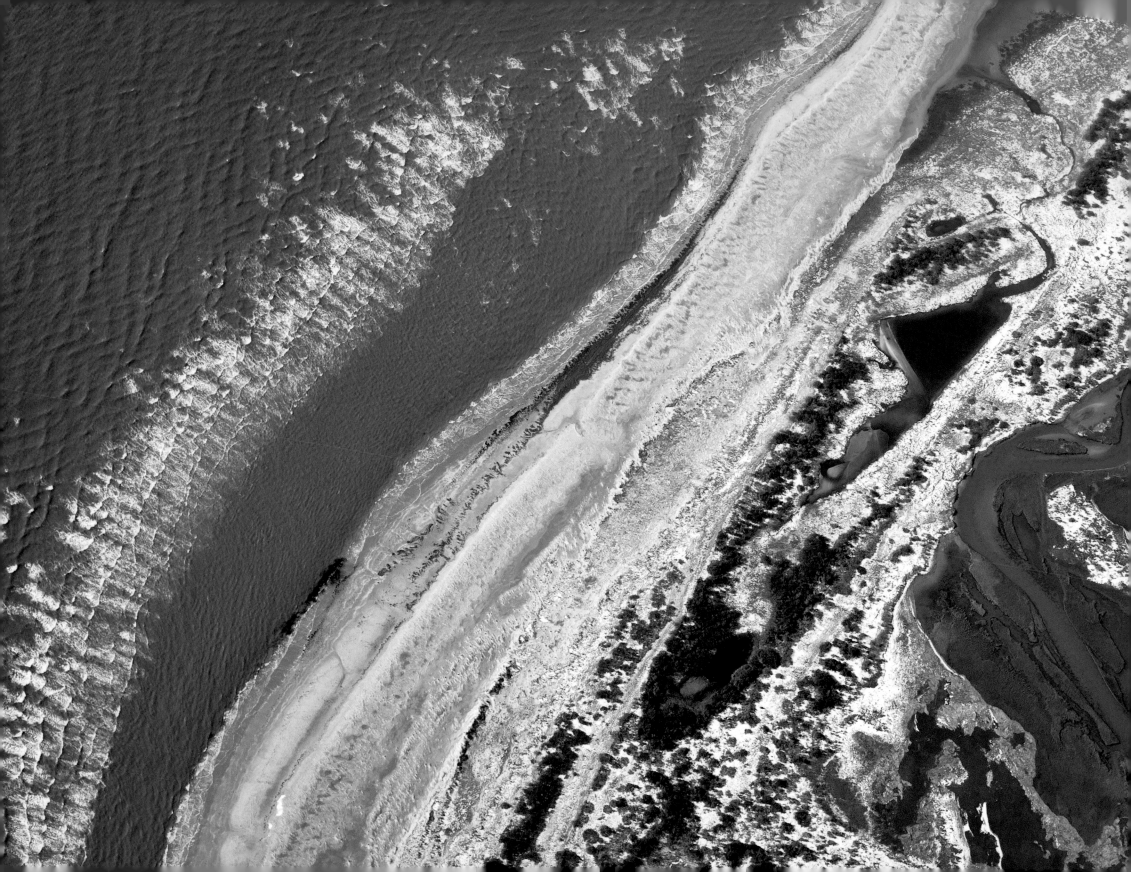

PRECEDING SPREAD, LEFT: White sand meets white caps on Tangier Island in midwinter.
PRECEDING SPREAD, RIGHT: Fisherman Island National Wildlife Refuge is the southern-most island on Virginia's Eastern Shore and is bisected by Route 13 and the Chesapeake Bay Bridge-Tunnel.

LEFT: Downtown Norfolk, Virginia lights up along the Elizabeth River at dusk.
RIGHT: Above Route 13 on the Chesapeake Bay Bridge-Tunnel, a southbound car disappears into the southern tunnel.

ABOVE: Tomatoes line fields at sunset near Warehouse Prong and Sandpiper Cove east of the Accomack County Airport.

RIGHT: The Chesapeake Bay looks west toward the mouth of the York River.

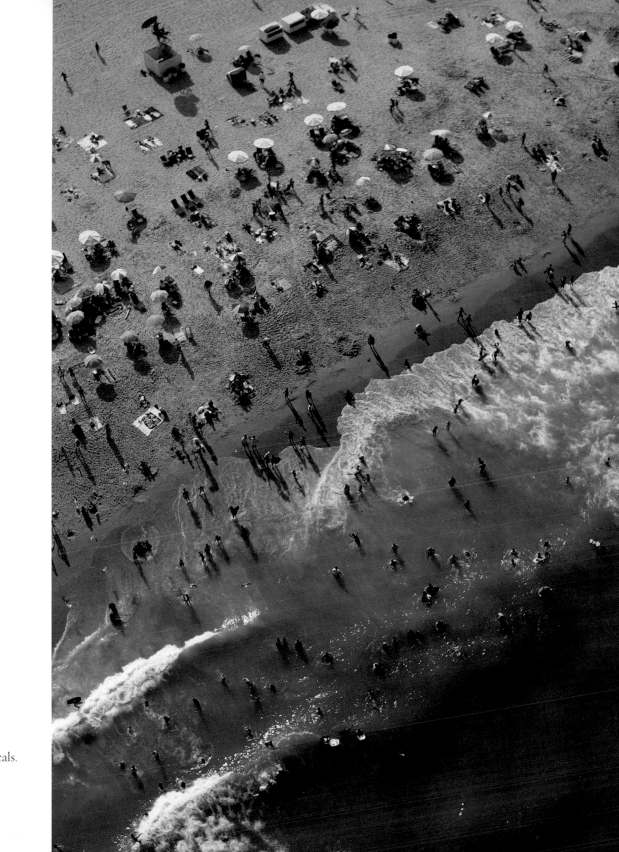

LEFT: A skimboarder catches a wave in early summer at Virginia Beach, Virginia.
RIGHT: Virginia Beach in midsummer is teeming with students, vacationers and locals.

LEFT: Craney Island, at the confluence of the James and Elizabeth Rivers in Portsmouth, Virginia, is constructed of dredge material from nearby shipping channels. It has become a critical habitat for threatened and endangered bird species: ospreys, least terns, piping plovers and brown pelicans.
ABOVE: The sun drops behind the frozen Chesapeake Bay from above the shoreline of Virginia's Eastern Shore.

PRECEDING PAGES: The Chesapeake Bay Bridge-Tunnel looks towards Virginia Beach.
LEFT: Flying Japan's flags, the 652-foot *Aegian Highway* cargo ship enters the Chesapeake Bay.

THANK YOU

CAMERON DAVIDSON

Aerial photography requires a partner in the air who can safely maneuver the helicopter or airplane into the perfect position so that I can capture the strongest image. The completion of this book would not have been possible without the contribution of many pilots and their willingness to preflight and takeoff before the sun broke the horizon.

I am grateful for the aerial skills of helicopter pilots Steve Bussmann of HeloFlights (MD 500); Andy Gibbs, Dave Hynes and Jonathan Guibas of Hampton Roads Helicopters (Robinson R22 and R44); Nicola Newland of HeloAir (Schweizer 300, Bell JetRanger); Mike Garland of Freedom Air (Bell JetRanger); Richard Harding of Lancaster Helicopters (MD 500); Larry Duppstadt (Bell JetRanger); and Keith Smith (Bell JetRanger). Fixed-wing pilots Dan Meyers (Cessna 172 STOL), Kevin Carpenter (Cessna 152) and Gary Livack (Cessna 177). Mike Langford, formerly of Capital Color in Arlington, Virginia, deserves a special round of applause for babysitting the vast quantities of E-6 color film processing during the early years of this project.

Sadie Quarrier of *National Geographic* tackled more than 20,000 frames and whittled the images to a manageable edit, a task that I never could have completed on my own. This book would not be possible without her efforts.

Alex Diaz, Heath Dwiggins, Regina Esposito, Gregg Glaviano, Richard Hamilton, Tom Kendzie, Kelsey de Sosta and Lynn Umemoto of Grafik Marketing Communications in Alexandria, Virginia went above and beyond the call of duty and friendship to design and produce this book.

Many thanks to David Fahrenthold of the *The Washington Post* who, on very short notice, wrote three wonderful summaries that capture the beauty and spirit of each region of the bay. Evan Jane Kriss and Jennifer Beeson Gregory of *The Washington Post Magazine* published an 18-page photo essay of my work, and I am indebted to them for their enthusiasm and dogged pursuit of the project.

Also thanks to Maggie Brett Kennedy of *Garden &Gun* magazine for her support and belief in the project by publishing a preview of the book. Special thanks to my friend Rich Dolesh of the National Recreation and Park Association for his advice and enthusiasm. Many thanks to John Echave for his belief in the project and to Richard Zamsky who mentored me in the beginning days of my career and whose advice I treasured. Special thanks are sent to Dr. Art Trask, Dr. Daniel Rooney, Dr. Wan Shin, Dr. Robert Reid, Dr. Jane Grayson, Dr. James Lamberti and Knox Singleton of Inova Health System.

Most of all, thank you to Linda for her steadfast trust and belief in me.

DAVID FAHRENTHOLD

David thanks Cameron for producing such a beautiful and meaningful body of work and for seeing a truly vast idea through to its conclusion. He thanks Lynda Robinson, *The Washington Post Magazine* editor who first connected him with Cameron, assigning him to write the text for a photo essay that appeared in the magazine. He thanks Chuck Epes of the Chesapeake Bay Foundation and Donald F. Boesch of the University of Maryland Center for Environmental Science for serving as expert sources. And he thanks his wife, Elizabeth Lewis, for being patient while he sat in the home office, evening after evening, trying to think of new synonyms for "pollution."

1.

2.

3.

1. Pilot Andy Gibbs in a Robinson R22 near Virginia Beach, Virginia.

2. Nicola Newland flying the HeloAir Schweizer 300 over central Virginia.

3. Lancaster Helicopters' MD 500 in Pennsylvania.

4.

5.

6.

4. Dave Hynes piloting his Robinson R44 over the Eastern Shore.

5. Steve Bussmann and his MD 500C.

6. Bussmann performs preflight at St. Mary's County Regional Airport in southern Maryland.

BIOGRAPHIES

CAMERON DAVIDSON

Davidson is an aerial and location portrait photographer based in Virginia. He shoots on assignment for a variety of print publications, such as *Vanity Fair, National Geographic, Preservation, Audubon, Smithsonian, Air and Space* and *Wired. Luerzer's Archive* recently named him one of the 200 best advertising photographers in the world. In addition to his commercial work, Davidson is a board member of the Community Coalition for Haiti and has been documenting the group's work in Haiti since 1999. His photography has been profiled in *Communication Arts, Studio, Photo/Design* and *Print* magazines. His work has won awards in the *Communication Arts Photo Annual, Graphis Photo, Print Regional Design Annual* and Pictures of the Year competition. Selected images from the bay project were recently featured as a cover article in the *The Washington Post Magazine* and in an online issue of *Garden & Gun.* Five books of his photography have been published: *A Moment of Silence: Arlington National Cemetery; Over Florida: A 'Wings Over America' Project; Washington D.C., Our Nation's Capital: An Aerial Portrait;* and *Washington DC from Above* and *Chicago from Above.*

DAVID FAHRENTHOLD

A native of Houston, Texas, Fahrenthold has worked for *The Washington Post* since 2000. He has covered the environment for five years, writing about the Chesapeake Bay, climate change, mountaintop coal mining and other topics both local and national. He has also covered the D.C. police department for the *Post* and spent one year as the paper's New England correspondent. Fahrenthold lives in Washington, D.C., with his wife, Elizabeth Lewis.

Copyright © 2011 by Cameron Davidson LLC.

399 Tennessee Avenue, Alexandria, Virginia 22305

Text © David Fahrenthold   Photography © Cameron Davidson

Photographs are available for exhibition, purchase and licensing at www.camerondavidson.com.

All Rights Reserved

ISBN: 978-0-9841620-0-0

Printed in China

Distributed by University of Virginia Press